Just Desserts

50 sweet surprises, with Fair Trade ingredients

© 2003

New Internationalist Publications™ Ltd,

55 Rectory Road, Oxford, OX4 1BW, UK

www.newint.org

New Internationalist is a registered trade mark

Design and editing contributions by Markus Bär, Max Havelaar

Foundation (Switzerland)

Recipe photos: Lotti Bebie, Zürich

Chapter heading images: Robert Schmid, www.3wimage.com

Litho: AZ Grafische Betriebe AG, Aarau

English language version editor: Troth Wells

English language translation produced by Translate-A-Book, Oxford

Printing and binding: Amadeus

Printed in Italy by Amadeus

*This book was first published by AT Verlag, Zürich, 2002, Switzerland,
in conjunction with Helvetas to mark the 10-year anniversary of the
foundation of Max Havelaar fair trade organization.*

ISBN 1 904456 06 5

Ralf Kabelitz

Just
Desserts

50 sweet surprises,
with Fair Trade ingredients

 Fair Trade Cookbooks

Unless stated otherwise, all recipes serve 4.

The baking times are based on conventional ovens.
The cooking time in fan-assisted ovens should be reduced
by a few minutes – check the manufacturer's instructions.

Where sugar and honey are listed, you may prefer to reduce
the amount. Brown or unrefined sugar and honey contain
more or less the same calories as refined sugar, and all are
equally tooth-rotting. *Glucose* which is also referred to as
dextrose is a moderately sweet sugar found in vegetables
and fruit. *Fructose*, also called *levulose* or fruit sugar, is
found associated with glucose in many fruits, as well as in
honey. *Sucrose* is one of the sweetest forms of sugars. It is
found in granulated, powdered, brown sugar and molasses
and also occurs naturally in a variety of fruits and vegetables.

Gelatin: 4 sheets of leaf gelatin are equal to 1 tablespoon of
granulated unsweetened gelatin. One envelope of granulated
gelatin = $1/4$ ounce = about $2^1/2$ teaspoons. Two non-animal
sources of thickening agent are Carrageen, a gelatinous
substance derived from seaweed and Agar (also agar-agar,
kanten and *Japanese gelatin*), a dried seaweed sold in blocks,
powder and strands that is used as a setting agent. Agar has
stronger setting properties than gelatin, so use less when
substituting.

Ice cream: several recipes use an ice–cream maker. If you do
not have one, see what to do on page 97.

Contents

Doubling the delight of desserts

We make desserts as a treat for our guests and ourselves. With these little confections we can break some of the rules of everyday life – once in a while we allow ourselves a bit more sugar and a few more calories.

The pleasure of anticipation begins with shopping. Should it be succulent and sweet? Or bitter-sweet? Do we fancy a light-as-air mousse, a fruity ice cream or sorbet or a substantial torte? Naturally, we choose the best and freshest ingredients and perhaps we make some minor changes to the recipe, indulging our creativity. During the careful preparation stages we are already wondering what dishes or plates will show our creation off to the best advantage and what decorations and flourishes will add an air of festivity.

And that's fine – of course we're entitled to indulge ourselves once in a while, relax, enjoy, escape from the mundane.

However, the mundane catches up with us soon enough. 'Cultivating cocoa means so much work for so little money,' says cocoa farmer Priscilla Asamoa of Ghana. Should we be sparing a thought for Mrs Asamoa as we enjoy a sweet treat? Yes! I promise you that you will get greater pleasure from the creative preparation of ingredients and enjoy your desserts more, if you know that the farmers and workers in the lands of the southern hemisphere have earned a fair income. This, too, is a change from the norm, as subsistence-level prices for tropical agricultural products are still the exception.

Priscilla Asamoa is lucky: 'Thanks to fair trade, at least we receive fair prices.' She works in the co-operative Kuapa Kokoo, which sells its products endorsed by the Max Havelaar fair trade certification. And Priscilla Asamoa thanks you, consumers who look for the fair trade label.

Paola Ghillani
Chief Executive Officer, Max Havelaar Foundation (Switzerland)

Honey and Sugar –

Sweetness from the South

Brazil, India, the EU, China, the US and Thailand are the world's largest sugar-growers – though not all of what they grow is exported. And who consumes the most? Brazilians – 128 pounds/58 kilos per person a year. Australians eat 108 pounds/49 kilos; in the EU it's 84 pounds/38 kilos and in the US, 75 pounds/34 kilos. Nearly all the sugar grown in Majority World countries is cane sugar, while in the North it is beet sugar.

Fair trade in sugar differs from that in coffee and cocoa because it has to contend with competition from Europe and the US. The EU protects beet sugar through subsidies and charges high tariffs on cane sugar from developing countries. In spite of these problems, fair-trade sugar can still be found in your fair-trade shop; otherwise purchase cane sugar.

Orange Blossom Honey Parfait

3 egg yolks
2 tablespoons clear orange blossom honey
1 tablespoon castor sugar
3 tablespoons orange liqueur
1¼ cups / 250 ml / 8 fl oz whipping cream
4 oranges, peeled and sliced

Whisk together the egg yolks, honey, sugar and liqueur in a heatproof bowl set over a pan of barely simmering water until thick and frothy.

Remove the bowl from the heat and immediately place in a bowl of iced water. Continue whisking until the mixture is cold.

Whip the cream until stiff, then gently fold it into the egg yolk mixture, without knocking out too much air. Transfer the mixture to a freezerproof mold or loaf tin and freeze for 3-4 hours.

To serve, loosen the parfait by dipping the base of the mold or loaf tin in warm water, then invert onto a plate. Cut it into slices, arrange on serving plates and decorate with the orange slices.

The orange blossom honey,
together with the orange liqueur,
gives this dessert a lovely fragrant flavor.

An easy-to-prepare, light delight for lovers of cheesecake.

Berry Cheesecake with Honey

Butter or margarine, for greasing
1¼ cups / 250 g / 9 oz low-fat curd cheese
2 tablespoons melted butter or margarine
3 tablespoons clear honey
grated rind and juice of 1 lemon
2 tablespoons arrowroot
3 eggs, separated
2 tablespoons vanilla sugar
1 cup / 150 g / 5 oz frozen mixed berries
2 tablespoons icing sugar

Preheat the oven to 180°C/350°F/Gas Mark 4. Grease a soufflé dish with butter.

Mix together the curd cheese, melted butter, honey, lemon rind and juice in a bowl. Stir in the arrowroot until combined, then beat in the egg yolks.

Whisk the egg whites in a clean grease-free bowl until soft peaks form. Gradually whisk in the vanilla sugar until stiff. Gently fold the egg whites into the cheese mixture.

Pour the mixture into the prepared soufflé dish, decorate with the berries and bake for 30 minutes. Sprinkle with the icing sugar and serve warm.

Tip:
This tastes wonderful served with a fruit or vanilla sauce.

Swiss Carrot Cake

6 eggs, separated
3/4 cup / 150 g / 5 oz soft brown sugar
grated rind and juice of 1 lemon
2 1/4 cups / 250 g / 9 oz ground hazelnuts
1/2 cup / 50 g / 2 oz ground almonds
2 cups / 300 g / 11 oz carrots, finely grated
pinch of ground cinnamon
1/2 cup / 50 g / 2 oz plain flour
1 cup / 50 g / 2 oz fresh breadcrumbs
2 teaspoons baking powder
1/3 cup / 65 g / 2 1/2 oz castor sugar
small marzipan carrots, to decorate

Glaze:
3/4 cup / 100 g / 3 3/4 oz icing sugar
2 tablespoons lemon juice

Preheat the oven to 180°C/350°F/Gas Mark 4.
Line an 11-in/28-cm cake tin with greaseproof paper.

Beat the egg yolks with the brown sugar in a
bowl until thick and pale.

Stir in the lemon rind and juice, ground
hazelnuts, ground almonds, carrots and cinnamon.

Mix together the flour, breadcrumbs and baking
powder in another bowl and add to the egg yolk
mixture.

Whisk the egg whites in a clean grease-free
bowl until soft peaks form. Gradually whisk in the
castor sugar until stiff, then gently fold the egg
whites into the cake batter.

...continued

Swiss Carrot Cake

Pour the batter into the prepared tin and smooth the surface. Bake for 50-60 minutes and then turn the cake out on to a wire rack to cool.

To make the glaze, blend the icing sugar with just enough of the lemon juice to make a pourable icing. Transfer the cake to a serving plate or cake stand and pour the glaze over it. Decorate with marzipan carrots and leave to set before serving.

Honey and Yogurt Mousse

Serves 6

1 1/3 cups / 300 ml / 1/2 pint full-fat natural yogurt
1/8 cup / 25 g / 1 oz castor sugar
1/3 cup / 100 g / 3 3/4 oz clear honey
1 teaspoon grated orange rind
juice of 1/2 lemon
4 gelatin leaves*
1 1/4 cups / 250 ml / 8 fl oz double or whipping cream

Mix together the yogurt, sugar, honey, orange rind and lemon juice in a bowl.

Soak the gelatin in a small bowl of cold water for 5 minutes, until softened. Remove the leaves from the bowl, squeeze out the excess water, then transfer to a heatproof bowl or small saucepan. Stand the bowl or pan in a large pan of simmering water and heat gently until the gelatin is liquid. Stir the liquid gelatin into the yogurt mixture and set aside to cool.

Whip the cream until stiff. As soon as the yogurt mixture begins to set, fold in the cream. Leave to cool and set for a further 1-2 hours.

*see recipe notes page 4

Ginger and honey — not only a perfect flavor combination, but also one with healing properties.

Honeyed Milk with Ginger

2-in/5-cm piece of fresh root ginger, peeled
and grated
2 cups / 500 ml / 18 fl oz milk
2-3 tablespoons clear honey

Put the ginger in a small pan, pour in the milk and bring to just below boiling point. Remove the pan from the heat and set aside to infuse for 10 minutes.
Blend in the honey and drink while hot.

The fastest home-made ice cream in the world.

Yogurt and Honey Ice Cream

2½ cups / 500 ml / 18 fl oz full-fat natural
yogurt
½ cup / 150 g / 5 oz clear honey

Mix the yogurt with the honey and freeze in an ice-cream maker*, following the manufacturer's instructions.

Tip:
If you wish, you could also flavor the yogurt with 7 tablespoons of fruit purée.

*If you do not have an ice-cream maker, see page 97   **15**

Soufflé Omelet with Honey and Mixed Berry Cheese

3 eggs, separated
1/8 cup / 25 g / 1 oz castor sugar
pinch of grated lemon rind
1 teaspoon arrowroot

Honey and mixed berry cheese:
1 1/4 cups / 250 g / 9 oz full-fat curd cheese
3 tablespoons clear honey
1 tablespoon castor sugar
1 teaspoon vanilla essence
1 3/4 cups / 250 g / 9 oz mixed berries or
    strawberries
7 tablespoons double or whipping cream
butter or margarine, for frying

Beat the egg yolks with the sugar and lemon rind in a bowl until pale and fluffy. Whisk the egg whites in a clean grease-free bowl until stiff, then gently fold into the egg yolk mixture. Sprinkle over the arrowroot and stir in.

To make the honey and mixed berry cheese, mix together the curd cheese, honey, sugar and vanilla in a bowl. Fold in the berries. Whip the cream in a separate bowl until stiff, then fold into the cheese mixture.

Melt a knob of butter in a frying pan, add a quarter of the egg mixture and cook to form a golden-yellow omelet. If you want to set the top surface of the omelet, hold it briefly under a preheated grill or place in a very hot oven for a few minutes.

Repeat with the remaining egg mixture to make four omelets. Fold the omelets in half and serve with the honey and mixed berry cheese.

Soufflé Omelet with Honey
and Mixed Berry Cheese

Honey Cake with Candied Orange Peel

2/3 cup / 150 g / 5 oz butter or margarine,
softened, plus extra for greasing
4 eggs
5/8 cup / 150 g / 5 oz dark syrup or treacle
1/3 cup / 100 g / 3 3/4 oz clear honey
2 tablespoons soft brown sugar
2 tablespoons rum
1 tablespoon mixed spice
2 1/2 cups / 300 g / 11 oz plain flour
2 teaspoons baking powder
1/4 cup / 50 g / 2 oz candied orange peel,
chopped

Preheat the oven to 160°C/325°F/Gas Mark 3.
Grease a 10-in /25-cm long loaf tin.

Cream the butter/margarine in a large bowl
until light and fluffy, then gradually beat in the
eggs. Beat in the syrup or treacle, honey, sugar, rum
and mixed spice.

Sift together the flour and baking powder into
another bowl, then gradually stir into the butter
mixture. Fold in the candied orange peel.

Pour the batter into the prepared tin and bake
for about 1 hour. Transfer to a wire rack to cool.

Honey Cake with Candied Orange Peel

Raspberry sauce always tastes wonderful – especially when it's served hot with honey and vanilla ice cream.

Honey and Vanilla Ice Cream with Hot Raspberry Sauce

Serves 10

Honey and vanilla ice cream:
2 vanilla pods
2$1/4$ cups / 500 ml / 18 fl oz double or
   whipping cream
2 cups / 500 ml / 18 fl oz milk
$1/2$ cup / 65 g / 2$1/2$ oz soft brown sugar
10 egg yolks
$1/2$ cup / 150 g / 5 oz clear honey

Hot raspberry sauce:
1$1/4$ cups / 300 ml / $1/2$ pint orange juice
$1/3$ cup / 65 g / 2$1/2$ oz castor sugar
6 cups / 1 kg / 2$1/4$ lb raspberries, fresh or frozen
$1/8$ cup / 20 g / $3/4$ oz arrowroot

Halve the vanilla pods lengthways, scrape out the seeds with the point of the knife and place the pods and seeds in a pan with the cream, milk and sugar. Bring just to the boil, stirring occasionally until the sugar has dissolved. Remove the pan from the heat and set aside to infuse for 10 minutes. Remove the vanilla pods.

Beat the egg yolks in a heatproof bowl. Add the milk and cream mixture while still hot, beating constantly with a whisk. Set the bowl over a pan of simmering water and stir constantly with a wooden spoon until the mixture thickens. Stir in the honey. Remove the bowl from the heat and place in iced water to cool. Freeze the mixture in an ice-cream maker following the manufacturer's instructions.

To prepare the raspberry sauce, pour the orange juice into a small pan, add the sugar and bring to the boil, stirring until the sugar has dissolved. Mix the arrowroot with a little cold water in a small bowl to make a smooth paste. Stir it into the pan and cook until the sauce has thickened slightly. Add the raspberries and bring back to the boil briefly. Serve the sauce hot over the vanilla ice cream.

Tip:
If you do not have an ice-cream maker, pour the mixture into a plastic container and place it in the freezer for 1 hour, or until ice crystals are beginning to form around the edge. Turn the mixture into a bowl and beat well to break up the crystals, then return it to the container and freeze again. Repeat the process twice more at hourly intervals, then return the ice cream to the freezer until solid.

A wonderfully light and refreshing summer flan.

Light Lemon Yogurt Flan

1¼ cups / 150 g / 5 oz plain flour
1 teaspoon baking powder
½ cup / 65 g / 2½ oz soft brown sugar
4 egg yolks
⅓ cup / 75 g / 3 oz butter or margarine, softened
1 teaspoon grated lemon rind
½ cup / 120 ml / 4 fl oz lemon juice
⅓ cup / 100 g / 3¾ oz orange blossom honey
8 gelatin leaves
1¾ cups / 400 ml / 14 fl oz natural yogurt
1⅓ cups / 300 ml / ½ pint whipping cream

Sift together the flour and baking powder into a bowl. Add the sugar, one egg yolk and the butter

...continued

and, using an electric mixer fitted with dough hooks, mix to a smooth dough. Leave to rest in the refrigerator for at least 30 minutes.

Preheat the oven to 200°C/400°F/Gas mark 6.

Roll out the dough between two pieces of Saran wrap/cling film and use to line a 10-in/25-cm round flan tin. Prick the dough all over with a fork and bake for 10 minutes. Remove the tin from the oven and leave to cool.

Beat the remaining egg yolks with the lemon rind, lemon juice and honey in a heatproof bowl set over a pan of simmering water for 5-10 minutes.

Soak the gelatin in a small bowl of cold water for 5 minutes, until softened. Remove the leaves from the bowl, squeeze out the excess water, then dissolve in the egg yolk mixture while it is still warm. Place the bowl in iced water and leave the mixture to cool. Stir in the yogurt.

Beat the cream until stiff and, as soon as the yogurt mixture begins to set, fold in the cream. Pour the mixture into the flan case and smooth the surface. Chill in the refrigerator for at least 2 hours.

Honey Sabayon

7 tablespoons sparkling white wine
4 egg yolks
1/4 cup / 50 g / 2 oz clear honey
lemon juice, to taste

Beat together the wine, egg yolks and honey in a heatproof bowl set over a pan of simmering water until thickened and increased in volume. Flavor with lemon juice to taste.

Tip:
This fluffy sauce goes beautifully with fruit sorbets.

Light Lemon Yogurt Flan

Fruit Minestrone with Elderflower Sauce

Sauce:
1 banana
1 lemon
7 tablespoons elderflower cordial
3/4 cup / 200 ml / 7 fl oz water
2/3 cup / 150 ml / 1/4 pint orange juice
3/8 cup / 75 g / 3 oz castor sugar

Minestrone:
5 cups / 800 g / 1 3/4 pounds assorted seasonal fruits,
   such as strawberries, apples, kiwi fruits, melon
2 tablespoons lemon juice
shredded fresh basil leaves, to decorate

Peel the banana and cut it into pieces. Peel the lemon, slice and remove the pips. Place the banana, lemon, elderflower cordial, water, orange juice and sugar in a blender or food processor and process to a purée.

Prepare the seasonal fruits and place in a large serving bowl. Add the lemon juice and elderflower sauce and mix well.

Decorate the fruit minestrone with the basil.

Tip:
Serve with Yogurt and Honey Ice Cream (see page 15).

Fruit Minestrone with Elderflower Sauce

Coffee –

The flavor for all seasons

The West's craving for coffee continues. The Finns put away the most coffee per head of population at 30 pounds/14 kilos. In the US and Canada it is around 9 pounds/4 kilos; UK 4 pounds/2 kilos, about the same as Australia. And all that coffee comes from the countries of the South – the biggest producers are Brazil, Colombia, Indonesia, Vietnam and Mexico.

In most producing countries, coffee cultivation was initiated by colonial powers to establish a source of revenues from exports. Many small coffee farmers today receive prices lower than the costs of production, forcing them into a cycle of poverty and debt. Fair trade for coffee farmers means community development, health, education and environmental stewardship.

Desserts made with coffee are a delight, guaranteed to please all sophisticated palates.

Coffee Mousse with Raspberry Sauce

1 cup / 250 ml / 8 fl oz milk
3 tbsp coffee beans
3 egg yolks
1/2 cup / 100 g / 3 3/4 oz castor sugar
3 1/2 gelatin leaves*
1 1/4 cups / 250 ml / 8 fl oz double or
    whipping cream
chocolate chips or chocolate coffee beans,
    to decorate

Raspberry sauce:
1 1/2 cups / 200 g / 7 oz raspberries
2 tbsp castor sugar
1/4 cup / 50 ml / 2 fl oz orange juice

Bring the milk to the boil in a small pan. Add the coffee beans, remove the pan from the heat and leave to infuse for 20 minutes. Strain the milk into a heatproof bowl.

Add the egg yolks and sugar, set over a pan of simmering water and beat until thickened and pale.

Soak the gelatin in a small bowl of cold water for 5 minutes, until softened. Remove the leaves from the bowl, squeeze out the excess water, then dissolve in the egg yolk mixture while it is still warm. Place the bowl into iced water and leave to cool, stirring occasionally.

Beat the cream until stiff and, as soon as the egg yolk mixture begins to set, gently fold it in.

Chill in the refrigerator.

...continued

*see recipe notes page 4

Coffee Mousse with Raspberry Sauce

Put the raspberries in a small pan and add the sugar and orange juice. Bring to the boil, then remove from the heat. Transfer the mixture to a blender or food processor and process to a purée. Next, push through a fine sieve into a bowl. Serve the sauce with the coffee mousse. Decorate the serving dish with chocolate chips or chocolate coffee beans.

Light Coffee Ice Cream

1 cup / 250 ml / 8 fl oz milk
1/4 cup / 50 g / 2 oz coffee beans
1 1/4 cups / 250 ml / 8 fl oz double cream
1 vanilla pod, slit open
5 egg yolks
1/2 cup / 100 g / 3 3/4 oz castor sugar
2 oz / 50 g / 2 oz milk chocolate, chopped

Bring the milk to the boil in a small pan. Add the coffee beans, remove the pan from the heat and leave to infuse for several hours. Strain into a clean pan.

Add the cream to the pan and bring to the boil. Add the vanilla pod, remove from the heat and leave to infuse for 10 minutes. Remove the vanilla pod.

Beat the egg yolks with the sugar until light and fluffy, then stir into the milk mixture. Cook over a medium heat, stirring constantly with a wooden spoon until the mixture thickens. Stand the pan in a bowl of iced water to cool completely.

Pour the mixture into an ice-cream maker and freeze following the manufacturer's instructions. Alternatively, freeze in a plastic container in the freezer, beating three times to break up the ice crystals (see page 97). Towards the end of the freezing process, stir in the chopped chocolate.

Tiramisù

4 egg yolks
¼ cup / 50 g / 2 oz castor sugar
2 gelatin leaves*
1¼ cups / 250 g / 9 oz mascarpone cheese
⅔ cup / 150 ml / ¼ pint whipping cream
20 sponge fingers
1 cup / 250 ml / 8 fl oz strong black coffee,
   cooled
5 tbsp brandy
2 tbsp cocoa powder, to decorate

Whisk the egg yolks and sugar with a hand whisk until pale and foamy.

Soak the gelatin in a small bowl of cold water for 5 minutes, until softened. Remove the leaves, squeeze out the excess water, then transfer to a heatproof bowl or small saucepan. Stand the bowl or pan in a large saucepan of simmering water and heat gently until the gelatin is liquid. Stir the liquid gelatin into the egg yolk mixture.

Add the mascarpone and beat until smooth.

Whip the cream until stiff, then gently fold it in.

Line the base of a soufflé dish with sponge fingers. Mix the coffee and brandy in a small bowl and pour over the biscuits. Leave to soak for a few minutes. Spread half the mascarpone mixture over them. Arrange the remaining biscuits on top and cover with the rest of the mascarpone mixture. Chill in the refrigerator for at least 2 hours.

Sift cocoa powder evenly over the top of the dessert, cut into portions and serve.

*see recipe notes page 4

Mascarpone and Coffee Cream with Berry Compote

Berry compote:
2 cups / 300 g / 11 oz mixed berries,
  such as strawberries, raspberries,
  bilberries, redcurrants, gooseberries
2/3 cup / 150 ml / 1/4 pint orange juice
1/4 cup / 50 g / 2 oz castor sugar
1/8 cup / 25 g / 1 oz arrowroot

Mascarpone and coffee cream:
11/3 cups / 300 g / 11 oz mascarpone cheese
11/3 cups / 300 g / 11 oz low-fat curd cheese
1/2 cup / 100 g / 3 3/4 oz castor sugar
4 tbsp lemon juice
4 tbsp strong black coffee, cooled
1 tsp vanilla essence
7 tbsp double cream, whipped
1/2 cup / 50 g / 2 oz pistachio nuts, chopped

First make the berry compote. Pour the orange juice into a small pan, add the sugar and bring to the boil, stirring until the sugar has dissolved. Mix the arrowroot with a little cold water to a smooth paste in a small bowl. Stir into the pan and boil, stirring constantly until slightly thickened. Stir in the berries, remove the pan from the heat and leave to cool.

To make the mascarpone and coffee cream, mix together the mascarpone, curd cheese, sugar, lemon juice, coffee and vanilla essence.

Spoon 2 tablespoons of berry compote, 2 tablespoons of mascarpone and coffee cream into each of four tall glasses or sundae dishes. Make

...continued

Mascarpone and Coffee
Cream with Berry Compote

33

more layers of compote and cream until the mixture is all used.

Decorate with whipped cream and chopped pistachio nuts before serving.

Delight and impress your friends with these tasty treats.

Coffee Eclairs
Makes 8-10

$1/2$ cup / 120 ml / 4 fl oz water
pinch of salt
1 tsp castor sugar
$1/4$ cup / 50 g / 2 oz butter or margarine
$3/4$ cup / 90 g / $3^1/2$ oz flour, sifted
2 eggs, lightly beaten
$3^3/4$ oz / 100 g / $3^3/4$ oz dark chocolate, melted

Filling:
$3/4$ cup / 200 ml / 7 fl oz milk
$1/4$ cup / 50 ml / 2 fl oz strong black coffee
2 egg yolks
$1/4$ cup / 50 g / 2 oz castor sugar
$1/8$ cup / 25 g / 1 oz arrowroot
7 tbsp double or whipping cream

Preheat the oven to 200°C/400°F/Gas Mark 6. Line a baking sheet with wax/greaseproof paper.

Pour the water into a pan and add the salt, sugar and butter. Heat until the butter has melted. Remove the pan from the heat and add the sifted flour all in one go. Stir vigorously with a wooden spoon. Return the pan to the heat and cook, stirring constantly, for 1 minute, until the mixture comes away from the side of the pan. Transfer the mixture to a bowl and leave to cool slightly, then gradually beat in the eggs, a little at a time.

Spoon the mixture into a piping bag and pipe the dough into fingers on the baking sheet. Bake for 15-20 minutes. Do not open the oven door during the first 10 minutes. Transfer the éclairs to a wire rack to cool.

To make the filling, pour the milk and coffee into a small pan and bring to the boil.

Beat together the egg yolks and sugar until pale and fluffy, then stir in the arrowroot. Stir the egg yolk mixture into the milk, return to the heat and gradually bring to the boil, stirring constantly until the mixture thickens. Remove from the heat and leave to cool.

Whip the cream until stiff and fold into the cooled mixture.

Slit the éclairs lengthways and divide the filling among them. Cover the tops of the éclairs with melted chocolate.

When coffee was first introduced to Europe there was resistance from the Church, which described it as the 'drink of Satan'. Then Pope Clement VIII (1536-1605) tried the devil's beverage for himself and found it so delicious that 'it would be a sin to leave it to the unbelievers'.

Bananas —

Rays of sunshine

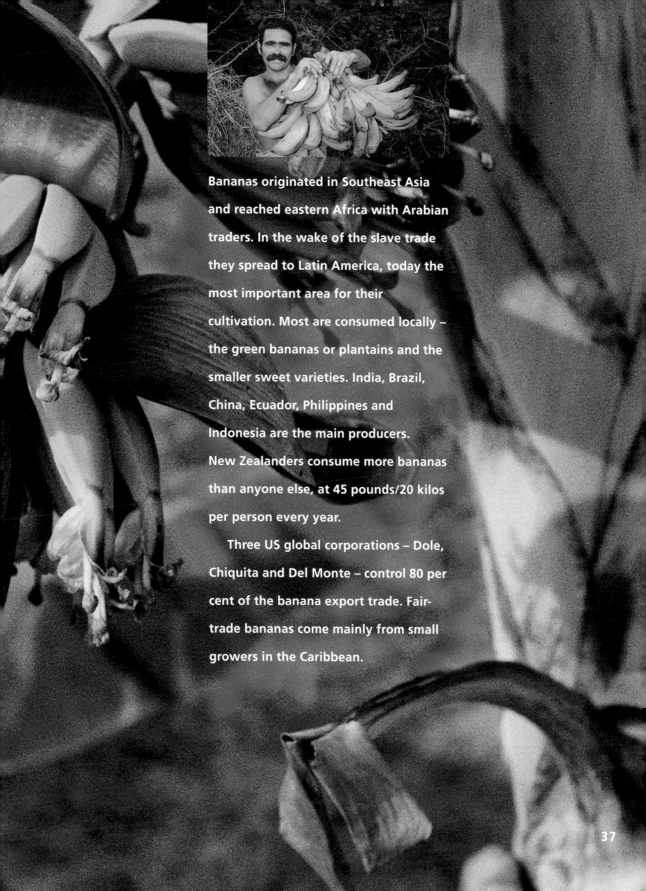

Bananas originated in Southeast Asia and reached eastern Africa with Arabian traders. In the wake of the slave trade they spread to Latin America, today the most important area for their cultivation. Most are consumed locally – the green bananas or plantains and the smaller sweet varieties. India, Brazil, China, Ecuador, Philippines and Indonesia are the main producers. New Zealanders consume more bananas than anyone else, at 45 pounds/20 kilos per person every year.

Three US global corporations – Dole, Chiquita and Del Monte – control 80 per cent of the banana export trade. Fair-trade bananas come mainly from small growers in the Caribbean.

Banana Mousse with Rhubarb Compote

Serves 6

3 gelatin leaves
3 bananas
5 tbsp lemon juice
7/8 cup / 185 g / 6 1/2 oz castor sugar
7 tbsp natural yogurt
2/3 cup / 150 ml / 1/4 pint orange juice
1 1/4 cups / 250 ml / 8 fl oz whipping cream
3 1/2 cups / 750 g / 1 lb 10 oz thin rhubarb,
    cut into 3-in / 2.5-cm chunks
1/8 cup / 25 g / 1 tsp arrowroot

Soak the gelatin in a small bowl of cold water for 5 minutes.

Meanwhile, peel and slice the bananas. Place them in a blender or food processor with the lemon juice, about half of the sugar, and the yogurt and process to a purée. Spoon the mixture into a bowl.

Heat 3 tablespoons of orange juice in a small pan. Remove the gelatin leaves from the bowl and squeeze out the excess water. Dissolve them in the warm orange juice, then stir into the banana purée. Set aside to cool.

Whip the cream until stiff. As soon as the banana purée is completely cool, gently fold it into the cream. Chill for 2-3 hours.

Place the rhubarb in a dish, sprinkle over the remaining sugar and set aside for 20 minutes to let the flavors expand.

...continued

Banana Mousse with
Rhubarb Compote

Bring the remaining orange juice to the boil, add the rhubarb and stir in the arrowroot. Simmer gently for a few minutes, stirring until thickened, then leave to cool.

To serve, take scoops of the mousse and arrange on serving plates with the rhubarb compote.

Banana Sorbet

1/4 cup / 50 ml / 2 fl oz water
1/4 cup / 50 g / 2 oz castor sugar
4 ripe bananas
1 tbsp lemon juice
3 tbsp coconut liqueur

Heat the water with the sugar in a small pan, stirring until the sugar has dissolved. Remove from the heat and leave to cool.

Peel the bananas and cut into chunks.

Pour the cooled syrup into a blender and add the bananas, lemon juice and liqueur to make a purée. Freeze in an ice-cream maker, following the manufacturer's instructions, or in a plastic container in the freezer, beating three times to break up the ice crystals (see page 97).

A beautifully smooth sorbet with coconut liqueur adding a touch of elegance.

Banana Spring Rolls

2 bananas
1 tbsp grated lemon rind
1 tbsp rum
2 tbsp soft brown sugar
4 spring roll wrappers, thawed if frozen
1 egg white, lightly beaten
vegetable oil, for deep-frying

Peel and halve the bananas.

Mix together the lemon rind, rum and sugar in a bowl.

Spread out the spring roll wrappers and brush the edges with egg white. Place half a banana on each wrapper and spoon over the rum mixture. Roll up the wrappers, tucking in the sides, to make neat parcels. Press gently to seal.

Heat the oil in a deep-fryer or large pan to 180-190°C/350-375°F or until a cube of day-old bread browns in 30 seconds. Lower the spring rolls into the oil and deep-fry until golden brown. Drain on kitchen paper and serve hot.

Tips:
Serve with Honey Sabayon (see page 22).

The calorie content of this recipe can be reduced by baking the banana rolls in a preheated oven, 180°C/350°F/Gas Mark 4, for 10 minutes, instead of deep-frying them.

Pancakes with Banana and Orange Filling

4 small bananas
1 tbsp / 15 g / ½ oz butter or margarine
2 tbsp soft brown sugar
6 tbsp orange juice
juice of ½ lemon
1 tbsp grated orange rind
vegetable oil, for frying
3 tbsp icing sugar, for sprinkling

Pancake batter:
1 cup / 115 g / 4 oz plain flour
½ cup / 120 ml / 4 fl oz milk
½ cup / 120 ml / 4 fl oz water
3 eggs
1 egg yolk
1 tbsp castor sugar
2 tbsp / 25 g / 1 oz clarified butter, melted

First make the pancake batter. Sift the flour into a bowl and stir in the milk and water to form a smooth batter. Stir in the eggs, egg yolk and sugar. Finally, stir in the melted clarified butter. Cover the batter and leave to stand for about 1 hour.

Peel and slice the bananas. Melt the butter/ margarine in a frying pan, add the banana slices and sprinkle with the brown sugar. Cook, stirring occasionally, until lightly browned, then pour in the orange and lemon juice and cook over a high heat for 1-2 minutes. Stir in the orange rind, remove the pan from the heat and set aside.

...continued

Pancakes with Banana
and Orange Filling

43

Heat a non-stick frying pan and brush with a little oil. Stir the batter, then add 2-3 tbsp to the pan. Tilt the pan to coat the base evenly and cook for 2-3 minutes, until the underside is golden. Flip the pancake over and cook for about 1 minute, until the second side is golden. Slide the pancake out onto a plate and keep warm, while you make more pancakes in the same way. Stack the pancakes interleaved with wax/greaseproof paper.

Fill two pancakes per serving with the banana filling while still warm and serve hot, sprinkled with icing sugar.

The botanical name for bananas is Musa paradisiaca – literally fruit of paradise. They combine many benefits: they are perfectly 'packaged', easy to peel, soft to chew, delicious, nutritious and easily digestible, and can be harvested all year round.

Flambéed Bananas

2 tbsp / 25 g / 1 oz butter
4 bananas, peeled and halved lengthways
1/3 cup / 75 g / 3 oz brown sugar
about 6 tbsp orange juice
juice of 1/2 lemon
1 tsp grated orange rind
4 tbsp orange liqueur
generous dash of rum

Melt the butter in a frying pan, add the bananas and cook until lightly browned on both sides. Sprinkle with the sugar and cook lightly. Pour in the orange juice, lemon juice and liqueur and cook over a high heat for a further 1-2 minutes.

To serve, heat the rum in a small pan or ladle, set light to it and pour over the bananas while flaming.

Tips:
Flambéeing always looks impressive, so why not bring the bananas, still flaming, to the table?

Serve with ice cream.

Orange juice –

The wake-up taste

Oranges taste fresh, sweet and exotic. We enjoy their vitamin-rich juice for breakfast, as an aperitif or just to drink, consuming around 15 quarts/15 liters each per year.

The Portuguese brought this fruit back from China in the 16th century. From Europe it was taken to the Americas. Brazil and the US account for about half the world production and about 80 per cent of the world's orange juice. In the other major producing countries – Mexico, China, Cuba, Spain, Greece, Italy, Morocco, South Africa – most oranges are for the fresh-fruit market. Fair trade can help small producers get markets for certified juice. And the pickers receive a fair wage, plus social-security contributions.

Pannacotta with Orange Sauce

1 vanilla pod
2½ cups / 500 ml / 18 fl oz double cream
⅓ cup / 65 g / 2½ oz castor sugar
3 gelatin leaves*
2 oranges, cut into slices to decorate

Orange sauce:
¾ cup / 200 ml / 7 fl oz orange juice
1 tsp arrowroot
2 tbsp orange blossom honey
2 tbsp orange liqueur

Slit the vanilla pod lengthways and scrape out the seeds. Mix the cream, sugar, vanilla pod and seeds in a small pan and bring to the boil. Remove the pan from the heat and leave to infuse for 10 minutes.

Soak the gelatin in a small bowl of cold water for 5 minutes. Remove the leaves from the bowl, squeeze out the excess water, then dissolve in the cream mixture while it is still warm.

Strain the mixture into a jug through a fine sieve. Pour into individual molds or coffee cups and chill in the refrigerator for several hours or overnight until set.

To make the sauce, bring the orange juice to the boil in a small pan. Mix the arrowroot with a little water to a smooth paste in a small bowl. Stir into the orange juice, bring back to the boil briefly and stir in the honey and orange liqueur. Pour into a bowl and when cold, chill in the refrigerator.

...continued

*see recipe notes page 4

Pannacotta with Orange Sauce

Loosen the pannacotta by briefly dipping the base of the molds in hot water, then invert on to serving plates. Decorate with orange slices and serve with the orange sauce.

A dream team – oranges and strawberries.

Orange Jelly with Strawberries

2 cups / 500 ml / 18 fl oz orange juice
3 tbsp castor sugar
juice of 1/2 lemon
8 gelatin leaves
1 1/2 cups / 250 g / 9 oz strawberries, quartered
icing sugar and strawberry leaves, to decorate
   (optional)

Pour the orange juice into a small pan, add the sugar and bring to the boil, stirring until the sugar has dissolved. Stir in the lemon juice. Remove the pan from the heat and set aside.

Soak the gelatin in a small bowl of cold water for 5 minutes. Remove the leaves from the bowl, squeeze out the excess water, then dissolve in the orange juice mixture while still hot. Leave to cool.

Divide the strawberries between four individual molds or coffee cups and pour over the cooled orange juice. Chill in the refrigerator until set.

To serve, briefly dip the base of the molds in hot water and invert on to serving plates, lightly dusted with icing sugar if using. Decorate with strawberry leaves, if you like, and any remaining strawberries.

Tip:
Serve with a cold vanilla sauce.

Orange Jelly with Strawberries

Campari and Orange Sorbet

2 cups / 500 ml / 18 fl oz orange juice
$^5/_8$ cup / 115 g / 4 oz castor sugar
2 tbsp grated orange rind
3 tbsp Campari
2 blood oranges, sliced, to decorate

Pour $^3/_8$ cup/100 ml/4 fl oz of the orange juice into a small pan and add the sugar. Bring to the boil, stirring until the sugar has dissolved. Add the orange rind, remove the pan from the heat and leave to cool.

Stir in the remaining orange juice and the Campari and freeze in an ice-cream maker following the manufacturer's instructions.

Serve the sorbet in tall wine glasses garnished with the orange slices.

A sweet and yet refreshingly fruity sauce to tickle the taste buds, this is the perfect accompaniment for many desserts.

Orange Butter Sauce

1$^1/_4$ cups / 300 ml / $^1/_2$ pint orange juice
$^1/_3$ cup / 115 g / 4 oz orange blossom honey
8 tbsp / 115 g / 4 oz butter, softened

Pour the orange juice into a small pan and add the honey. Bring to the boil, stirring constantly until the mixture has a syrupy consistency. Remove from the heat and cool to about 40°C/104°F.

Beat the butter and gradually add the orange juice, beating well after each addition.

…continued

Campari and Orange Sorbet

Do not store the sauce in the refrigerator, as it will become too hard.

Tip:
This sauce is an excellent accompaniment for dark or white chocolate mousse.

Orange Chiffon Cake

Butter or margarine, for greasing
2 cups / 225 g / 8 oz plain flour
pinch of salt
2 tsp baking powder
$7/8$ cup / 185 g / $6^1/_2$ oz castor sugar
grated rind of 2 oranges
$2/3$ cup / 150 ml / $1/_4$ pint orange juice
4 tbsp lemon juice
7 tbsp vegetable oil
4 eggs, separated

Preheat the oven to 160°C/325°F/Gas Mark 3. Grease a 10-in/25-cm long loaf tin with butter/margarine.

Sift together the flour, salt and baking powder into a bowl and stir in the sugar. Add the orange rind, orange juice, lemon juice, oil and egg yolks and mix well.

Whisk the egg whites in a clean grease-free bowl until stiff, then gently fold into the flour mixture. Spoon into the prepared tin and bake for 60-70 minutes. Turn out on to a wire rack to cool.

Strawberries are always a delight in themselves. All the more so if you add that certain something.

Strawberries with Orange Caramel

$^1/_3$ cup / 65 g / 2$^1/_2$ oz castor sugar
$^2/_3$ cup / 150 ml / $^1/_4$ pint orange juice
2 tbsp finely chopped orange rind
3 cups / 500 g / 1$^1/_4$ lb strawberries, halved
3 tbsp orange liqueur
3 fresh mint sprigs, shredded to decorate

Heat the sugar in a heavy-based pan until it melts and turns golden brown. Pour in the orange juice and cook, stirring until thoroughly combined. Stir in the orange rind, remove from the heat and leave to cool.

Divide the strawberries among individual plates, pour over the orange caramel and the liqueur and decorate with the mint.

Tip:
Serve with a scoop of vanilla ice cream or Pannacotta (see page 48).

Here's a treat using plump,
blue, really ripe, aromatic figs.

Orange Figs

12 ripe blue figs
thinly pared rind of 1 orange
2 cups / 500 ml / 18 fl oz orange juice
¼ cup / 50 g / 2 oz castor sugar
1 tbsp lemon juice
3 tbsp clear honey

Thinly peel the skin from the figs (if this is too difficult, do not peel the figs, but make four or five vertical slits to allow the syrup to penetrate better).

Cut the orange rind into fine strips with a sharp knife.

Pour the orange juice into a small pan, add the sugar and bring to the boil over a low heat, stirring constantly until the sugar has dissolved. Add the orange rind strips, lemon juice and honey.

Arrange the figs side by side in a suitable dish and pour the syrup over them. Leave, preferably overnight, for the syrup to penetrate.

Tip:
Serve with vanilla ice cream or Tea Crèmes (see page 66).

Orange Figs

Tea –

A refreshing pick-me-up

Tea, cultivated from early times in China and India as a health-giving stimulant, is a classic colonial product. The tea plantations in India and Sri Lanka are a legacy of the British Empire.

Some fair trade organizations have prioritized plantation workers rather than small farmers. The additional money obtained from fair-trade prices goes to help tea-pickers improve their lives and working conditions.

There are many different varieties, each with its own distinctive flavor. Ceylon teas are usually pale and delicately flavored, while Indian teas are generally richer in both color and flavor. Green tea, or gunpowder tea, is very fragrant and pale greenish-yellow. All these teas give a subtle and sophisticated flavor to these desserts.

A delicate and attractive dish
to delight your guests with.

Darjeeling Jelly
Serves 6

2 cups / 500 ml / 18 fl oz water
2-3 tbsp Darjeeling tea leaves
1/2 cup / 100 g / 3 3/4 oz sugar
3 tbsp orange liqueur
juice of 2 lemons
9 gelatin leaves*
2 cups / 300 g / 11 oz prepared fruit, such as
    halved grapes, raspberries, diced apple
7 tbsp double cream
1/2 tsp vanilla sugar

Bring the water to the boil, pour over the tea in a
pot or jug, cover and leave to infuse for 3-5
minutes. Strain into a bowl.

Stir in the sugar, orange liqueur and lemon juice.

Soak the gelatin in a small bowl of cold water
for 5 minutes. Remove the leaves from the bowl,
squeeze out the excess water, then dissolve in the
tea mixture.

Divide the fruit among six individual molds or
coffee cups and spoon in a little of the tea mixture.
Leave to cool until the jelly begins to set, then
spoon in the remaining tea mixture. Chill in the
refrigerator until set.

Beat the cream with the vanilla sugar until soft
peaks form.

To serve, briefly dip the base of the molds in
warm water, invert on to plates and serve with the
vanilla cream.

Tip:
*You can substitute 1 tsp agar-agar for the gelatin.
Follow the packet instructions for dissolving.
See also recipe notes page 4.

Darjeeling Jelly

The fact that the 'Red Bull' drink is effective but doesn't taste too good is no secret any more. 'Green Bull' is both effective and delicious.

Green Bull

2¹/₄ cups / 500 ml / 18 fl oz natural yogurt
¹/₃ cup / 130 g / 4¹/₂ oz clear honey
³/₄ cup / 200 ml / 7 fl oz water
2 tsp green tea leaves
¹/₂ cup / 100 g / 3 ³/₄ oz sugar
2 tbsp lemon juice
5 cups / 800 g / 1³/₄ lb fresh fruit salad

Mix the yogurt with the clear honey in a bowl, then freeze in an ice-cream maker following the manufacturer's instructions.

Bring the water to the boil, pour over the tea in a pot or jug, cover and leave to infuse the tea for 4-5 minutes. Strain into a bowl.

Stir in the sugar and leave to cool.

Stir in the lemon juice and pour over the fruit salad. Serve with the yogurt sorbet.

Iced Tea Sorbet

2 cups / 500 ml / 18 fl oz water
2-3 tbsp Darjeeling tea leaves
1/2 cup / 100 g / 3 3/4 oz sugar
juice of 2 lemons
4 tbsp orange liqueur

Bring the water to the boil, pour over the tea in a pot or jug, cover and leave to infuse for 3-4 minutes. Strain into a bowl.

Stir in the remaining ingredients until the sugar has dissolved, then leave to cool.

Freeze in an ice-cream maker following the manufacturer's instructions or in a plastic container in the freezer (see page 97).

Tip:
This sorbet may be served between courses to cleanse the palate during a formal dinner party.

Spiced Tea

1 tsp cardamom seeds, crushed
1 cinnamon stick, broken into small pieces
1 tsp / 20 g / 3/4 oz fresh root ginger, cut into thin strips
1 quart / 1 liter / 1 3/4 pints water
5 tsp Ceylon tea leaves

Put all the spices in a pan with the water and bring to the boil. Add the tea leaves, cover and set aside to infuse for 4 minutes. Filter through a fine strainer.

Not many people realize that tea
is a superb flavoring for desserts.

Ceylon Tea Parfait

3/4 cup / 200 ml / 7 fl oz water
5 tsp Ceylon tea leaves
7 tbsp milk
1 tsp finely grated orange rind
5 egg yolks
7/8 cup / 185 g / 6 1/2 oz soft brown sugar
4 tbsp rum
1 1/3 cups / 300 ml / 1/2 pint double cream

Bring the water to the boil, pour it over the tea in a pot or jug, cover and leave to infuse for 4-5 minutes. Strain into a pan. Bring to the boil again. Remove from the heat and stir in the orange peel.

Beat the egg yolks with the sugar in a heatproof bowl until pale and fluffy. Whisk in the tea mixture and the rum, set over a pan of barely simmering water and beat until thickened. Place in iced water and continue to beat until the mixture is cold.

Whip the cream until stiff in another bowl, then fold it in.

Transfer the mixture to a rectangular cake tin and place in the freezer overnight.

Tip:
Mango sauce makes an excellent accompaniment.

Ceylon Tea Parfait

Tea Crèmes

Serves 6

    3/4 cup / 150 g / 5 oz castor sugar
    1 cup / 250 ml / 8 fl oz water
    1 tbsp Ceylon tea leaves
    1 1/4 cups / 250 ml / 8 fl oz double cream
    3 eggs
    2 egg yolks

Preheat the oven to 150°C/300°F/Gas Mark 2. Reserve 1/4 cup/50 g/2 oz of the sugar and put the remainder in a heavy-based pan with 3-4 tablespoons water. Bring to the boil over a low heat, stirring constantly until the sugar has dissolved. Continue to boil, without stirring, until the syrup turns a pale golden color. Divide among six individual glass or china molds.

Bring the measured water to the boil, pour over the tea in a pot or jug, cover and leave to infuse for 3-4 minutes. Strain into a pan.

Add the cream and bring to just below boiling point. Remove the pan from the heat.

Beat together the eggs, egg yolks and reserved sugar. Gradually beat in the tea mixture. Strain and divide among the moulds.

Place the molds in a roasting tin and add enough water to come halfway up their sides. Bake for 20-25 minutes. If necessary to prevent the water from boiling, add a little cold water during cooking.

Turn off the heat, but leave the molds in the oven for a further 10 minutes. Remove the molds from the roasting tin and leave to cool.

To serve, loosen the edges with a small knife and invert on to plates.

Tip:
Serve with Orange Figs (see page 56).

When dissolving the sugar for the caramel, try not to splash the sides of the pan as you stir. Splashes encourage sugar crystals to form and they, in turn, encourage crystals to form in the caramel, spoiling its texture. Similarly, do not be tempted to stir the boiling syrup as this also causes crystals to form.

Green Tea Syrup with Rose Flowers

1 quart / 1 liter / 1¾ pints water
1 tbsp / 25 g / 1 oz dried rose flowers
2 tsp green tea leaves
2 cups / 500 g / 1¼ lb castor sugar
juice of 2 lemons

Bring the water to the boil, add the rose flowers and green tea and leave to infuse for 4 minutes. Strain the tea into a pan through a fine strainer. Add the sugar and reheat, stirring until it has dissolved. As soon as the sugar has fully dissolved, add the lemon juice.

Pour into a sterilized bottle, seal and store in a cool place.

Tip:
Makes a refreshing drink diluted with water or mineral water, a fine aperitif mixed with dry white wine or sparkling wine, or can be used to add a delicate flavor to creamy desserts and fruits, as in the following recipe.

Peaches in Green Tea and Rose Syrup

5 cups / 1 kg / 2¼ lb peaches
1 cup / 400 ml / 14 fl oz Green Tea Syrup with
    Rose Flowers (see page 67)
¾ cup / 200 ml / 7 fl oz dry white wine
3 lemon slices
1 vanilla pod

Make an incision around each peach, place in boiling water for 10 seconds, plunge into cold water and peel off the skins. Halve the peaches, remove the stones and cut each half into three pieces.

Bring the green tea syrup to the boil with the white wine. Add the lemon slices. Slit the vanilla pod and scrape out the seeds. Add the vanilla pod and seeds to the green tea mixture. Add the peach slices and simmer for 10 minutes.

Tip:
Serve with a scoop of vanilla ice cream.

Peaches in Green Tea and Rose Syrup

Tea Punch with Sparkling Wine
8-12 servings

2 cups / 500 ml / 18 fl oz water
4 heaped tsp Ceylon tea leaves
2 oranges, peeled, halved and thinly sliced
1 pink grapefruit, peeled, halved and thinly
    sliced
3 tbsp brown sugar
5 tbsp orange liqueur
2 tbsp white rum
2 bottles sparkling white wine, chilled
rose petals, to decorate (optional)

Bring the water to the boil, pour over the tea in a pot or jug, cover and leave to infuse for 4 minutes. Strain and pour into an ice cube tray. When cold, place in the freezer until set.

Place the orange and grapefruit slices in a large bowl and sprinkle with the sugar. Pour the liqueur and rum over them and leave to soak for several hours.

When ready to serve, pour the sparkling wine over the fruit and add the tea ice cubes. Decorate with rose petals if you like.

Tea Punch with
Sparkling Wine

Chocolate and Cocoa –

Legacy of the Maya and Aztecs

Cocoa originated in South America but was first cultivated by the Maya people in Central America. They and the Aztecs used it as a form of currency, and it also had religious significance.

The Spanish conquerors brought the beans to Europe and some 200 years later the first chocolate factory opened, in 1728. Today chocolate is big business. The Swiss eat the most at over 22 pounds/ 10 kilos each a year. In the UK it's 17 pounds/8 kilos while in Australia and the US the figure is 13 pounds/6 kilos.

Côte d'Ivoire is the world's largest producer, followed by Ghana and then Indonesia. Britain's Fairtrade Foundation says that sales of fair-trade products, including chocolate and cocoa, have grown by an average of 65 per cent every year.

Although not strictly speaking chocolate,
as it contains no cocoa solids, white chocolate
is hugely popular because it is so sweet.

White Chocolate Mousse with Caramelized Kumquats

Serves 8

> 9 oz / 250 g / 9 oz white chocolate, broken
>   into pieces
> 4 gelatin leaves
> 5 tbsp water
> 5 egg yolks
> 2-3 tbsp orange liqueur
> 2½ cups / 500 ml / 18 fl oz whipping cream
> ¼ cup / 50 g / 2 oz castor sugar
> 7 tbsp orange juice
> 4 / 200 g / 7 oz kumquats

Melt the chocolate in a heatproof bowl set over a pan of barely simmering water. Remove from the heat and set aside.

Soak the gelatin in a small bowl of cold water for 5 minutes.

Meanwhile, beat the egg yolks with the orange liqueur in a heatproof bowl set over a pan of barely simmering water until frothy. Remove the gelatin leaves from the bowl, squeeze out the excess water, then dissolve in the warm egg mixture. Add the melted chocolate and stir well. Leave the mixture to cool in the refrigerator for 10-15 minutes.

Whip the cream until stiff and gently fold it into the cooled egg mixture. Chill for 1 hour.

Heat the sugar in a heavy-based pan until it melts and turns golden brown. Add the orange

...continued

White Chocolate Mousse
with Caramelized Kumquats

juice and boil until the caramel has dissolved. Remove from the heat.

Quarter the kumquats and soak in the caramel syrup for 5 minutes

Scoop spoonfuls of the white chocolate mousse into bowls or glasses and serve garnished with the kumquats.

Tips:
If you use white chocolate cake covering instead of white chocolate, 2 gelatin leaves will be sufficient.

Dark – strong – irresistible – pure chocolate.

Chocolate Sorbet

2 cups / 500 ml / 18 fl oz water
$^1/_2$ vanilla pod
$^5/_8$ cup / 115 g / 4 oz castor sugar
$^1/_8$ cup / 25 g / 1 oz cocoa powder
5 oz / 150 g / 5 oz dark chocolate, broken
  into pieces

Bring the water to the boil. Slit the vanilla pod, scrape out the seeds and add these to the boiling water with the sugar and cocoa powder. Remove from the heat and leave to cool slightly. Whisk vigorously.

Whisk in the chocolate until it has melted. Freeze in an ice-cream maker* following the manufacturer's instructions.

*If you do not have an ice-cream maker, see page 97.

*Rich and wickedly indulgent,
this would be a perfect finale
to the meal.*

Caramelized Figs with Frothy Chocolate Sauce

$^1/_3$ cup / 75 g / 3 oz castor sugar
7 tbsp red wine
7 tbsp ruby port
7 tbsp orange juice
1 vanilla pod
1 clove
1 cinnamon stick
8 figs

Chocolate sauce:
$^3/_4$ cup / 200 ml / 7 fl oz milk
3 egg yolks
$^3/_8$ cup / 75 g / 3 oz soft brown sugar
2 tbsp whisky
3 tbsp drinking chocolate powder

Heat the castor sugar in a heavy-based pan until it melts and turns golden brown.

Pour in the wine, port and orange juice. Slit open the vanilla pod and add to the syrup with the clove and cinnamon stick. Boil for 10 minutes.

Make $^1/_2$-$^3/_4$ in/1-2 cm lengthways cuts in the figs, add to the syrup and simmer for 10 minutes. Heat the grill. Remove the figs with a slotted spoon, roll in the remaining sugar and place in a flameproof dish. Flash under a preheated grill to caramelize.

To make the chocolate sauce, whisk together the milk, egg yolks and sugar in a heatproof bowl set over a pan of barely simmering water until thick

...continued

and frothy. Stir in the whisky and chocolate powder.
Serve immediately with the caramelized figs.

Tip:
Serve with a scoop of Honey and Vanilla Ice Cream
(see page 20).

*There are innumerable recipes
for chocolate mousse. This version
is especially light and delicious.*

Dark Chocolate Mousse
Serves 6

7 oz / 200 g / 7 oz dark chocolate, broken
   into pieces
$\frac{1}{2}$ cup / 120 ml / 4 fl oz strong black coffee
4 eggs, separated
$\frac{1}{8}$ cup / 25 g / 1 oz vanilla sugar
$\frac{5}{8}$ cup / 120 ml / 4 fl oz double cream
$\frac{1}{4}$ cup / 50 g / 2 oz castor sugar

Melt the chocolate in a heatproof bowl set over a
pan of barely simmering water. Stir in the coffee.
Remove the bowl from the heat.

Whisk the egg yolks with the vanilla sugar in
another bowl until frothy, then stir into the
chocolate mixture.

Whisk the cream until stiff and gently fold into
the chocolate mixture.

Finally, whisk the egg whites with the sugar
until stiff in a clean grease-free bowl. Gently fold

into the chocolate mixture. Spoon into a serving
bowl or individual dishes and chill in the
refrigerator for several hours.

Quick Chocolate Cream Sauce

1 cup / 200 ml / 7 fl oz single cream
7 oz / 200 g / 7 oz dark chocolate, broken
   into pieces

Heat the cream in a pan, but do not allow it to boil.
   Add the chocolate and whisk gently until it has
melted completely.

Tip:
This goes beautifully with Honey and Vanilla Ice
Cream (page 20) or Banana Sorbet (page 40).

These soufflés are great — they don't collapse when you take them out of the oven.

Chocolate Soufflés with Almonds

8 tbsp / 100 g / 3 3/4 oz butter or margarine,
  plus extra for greasing
3 3/4 oz / 100 g / 3 3/4 oz dark chocolate with
  almonds, broken into pieces
4 egg yolks
1/3 cup / 75 g / 3 oz castor sugar
1/4 cup / 50 g / 2 oz plain flour, sifted
2 egg whites
7 tbsp double cream, whipped
2 fresh mint sprigs, to decorate

Preheat the oven to 180°C/350°F/Gas Mark 4.
Grease four individual soufflé dishes with
butter/margarine.

Melt the chocolate with the butter in a
heatproof bowl over a pan of barely simmering
water, stirring constantly. Remove from the heat.

Beat the egg yolks with half the sugar until
frothy, then gradually stir into the chocolate
mixture alternating with the flour.

Whisk the egg whites with the remaining sugar
until stiff in a clean grease-free bowl and gently
fold into the chocolate mixture. Spoon into the
prepared dishes.

Place the dishes in a roasting tin and add hot
water to come about halfway up their sides. Bake
for 30 minutes.

Transfer the soufflés to individual plates and
serve with a little whipped cream, decorated with
mint sprigs.

...continued

Chocolate Soufflés
with Almonds

Tips:
You can prepare the soufflé mixture the previous day and store it overnight in the soufflé dishes in the freezer. Thaw before baking.

Baking in a water-bath ensures that the soufflés cook evenly.

Baked Chocolate Creams
Serves 6

3/8 cup / 75 g / 3 oz castor sugar
1 vanilla pod
1 1/4 cups / 300 ml / 1/2 pint milk
1 cup / 200 ml / 7 fl oz double cream
1 tsp instant coffee granules
2 oz / 50 g / 2 oz dark chocolate
1 egg
3 egg yolks
7 tbsp whipping cream

Preheat the oven to 180°C/350°F/Gas Mark 4. Place the sugar in a heavy-based pan with 1 tbsp water. Bring to the boil, stirring until the sugar has dissolved, then boil, without stirring, until golden brown. Slit the vanilla pod and add to the pan with the milk and cream. Bring back to the boil, add the instant coffee and chocolate and stir until the chocolate has melted and the coffee has dissolved.

Remove the vanilla pod, strain the chocolate mixture through a fine sieve and stir in the egg and egg yolks.

Pour the mixture into six individual soufflé dishes and place them in a roasting tin. Add hot water to come about halfway up their sides. Bake for 20 minutes. If necessary to prevent the water from boiling, add a little cold water to the tin.

Remove the dishes from the water bath and leave to cool.

Whip the cream until stiff and serve with the cooled desserts.

Incredibly chocolaty, but not too heavy, and quick to prepare – wonderful.

Hazelnut and Chocolate Torte

1¹/₂ sticks / 150 g / 5 oz butter or margarine, diced, plus extra for greasing

¹/₄ cup / 50 g / 2 oz plain flour, plus extra for dusting

7 oz / 200 g / 7 oz dark chocolate, broken into pieces

1¹/₂ cups / 200 g / 7 oz ground hazelnuts

2 tsp baking powder

6 eggs

4 tbsp rum

³/₄ cup / 150 g / 5 oz unrefined sugar

3³/₄ oz / 100 g / 3³/₄ oz dark chocolate cake covering, melted

2 tbsp cocoa powder, sifted

Preheat the oven to 180°C/350°F/Gas Mark 4. Grease and flour a cake tin.

Melt the chocolate in a heatproof bowl set over a pan of barely simmering water. Remove from the heat and gradually whisk in the butter/margarine. Set aside.

Mix together the ground hazelnuts, flour and baking powder.

...continued

Beat together the eggs, rum and sugar in another bowl until frothy, then fold into the chocolate blend. Gradually stir in the flour mixture.

Spoon the mixture into the prepared cake tin, smooth the surface and bake for 50-60 minutes.

Turn out the cake onto a wire rack to cool. Cover the top with the chocolate cake covering and dust with cocoa powder.

Praline Parfait with Vanilla Cream
Serves 6-8

1/2 cup / 120 ml / 4 fl oz milk

3 egg yolks

3/8 cup / 75 g / 3 oz castor sugar

2 tbsp brandy

2 oz / 50 g / 2 oz praline chocolate, broken into pieces

3³/4 oz / 100 g / 3³/4 oz dark chocolate, broken into pieces

1³/4 cups / 400 ml / 14 fl oz whipping cream

1/4 cup / 25 g / 1 oz vanilla sugar

Bring the milk to the boil, then remove from the heat. Beat the egg yolks with the sugar in a heatproof bowl until pale and frothy. Add the milk, set the bowl over a pan of barely simmering water and stir with a wooden spoon until the mixture thickens. Add the brandy and remove from the heat.

Add the chocolate, stirring into the warm egg mixture until melted. Leave to cool, but don't place in the refrigerator.

...continued

Praline Parfait
with Vanilla Cream

85

Whip 1¼ cups/250 ml/8 fl oz of the cream until stiff. When the egg mixture is almost cold, fold in the cream. Spoon the mixture into a parfait mold or loaf tin and place in the freezer for a few hours, until frozen.

Beat the remaining cream with the vanilla sugar until stiff and serve with the parfait.

Cocoa was thought to be an aphrodisiac by the Mayans and Aztecs. It is now known that chocolate initiates a chain reaction which increases serotonin levels, stimulating feelings of happiness.

Chocolate Ice Cream with Rum and Raisins

1/2 cup / 50 g / 2 oz raisins
1/4 cup / 50 ml / 2 fl oz rum
4 egg yolks
1/2 cup / 100 g / 3 3/4 oz castor sugar
1 vanilla pod
1 cup / 250 ml / 8 fl oz milk
1 1/4 cups / 250 ml / 8 fl oz double cream
2 oz / 50 g / 2 oz dark chocolate, broken
    into pieces

Place the raisins in a small bowl, add the rum and leave to soak overnight. Remove the raisins, chop and drain well. Reserve the rum.

Beat the egg yolks with the sugar until creamy.

Slit the vanilla pod lengthways, place in a pan with the milk and cream and bring to the boil. Remove from the heat and set aside to infuse for 5 minutes. Add to the egg yolk mixture, return to the pan and stir with a wooden spoon over a medium heat until thickened. Do not allow it to boil.

Remove the pan from the heat and stir in the chocolate until melted. Stir in the raisins and 2 tbsp of the reserved rum. Freeze in an ice-cream maker following the manufacturer's instructions. If you don't have an ice-cream maker, see page 97.

Rice –

Going with the grain

Rice is the staple diet of more than half of the world's people. The main type eaten today probably originated in Asia where more than 90 per cent of the world's harvest is produced, mainly from small farmers. A type of rice from West Africa is less prolific but more resistant to drought and weeds. The main exporters are Thailand, Vietnam, US, India, China and Pakistan. The most rice is eaten in Southeast Asia (240-400 pounds/110-180 kilos per person per year).

For the farmers of Surin in northeast Thailand, fair trade support has helped access the international market and they are now beginning to benefit. Export-quality Surin rice and Basmati rice from India are distributed by fair-trade organizations in Europe.

*Rice puddings may remind
you of schooldays, but wait
until you've tried these delights…*

Bavarois with Rice and Oranges

Serves 6

3 cups / 750 ml / 1¼ pints water
½ cup / 100 g / 3¾ oz long grain rice
1 vanilla pod
2 cups / 500 ml / 18 fl oz milk
¾ cup / 175 g / 6 oz castor sugar
1 tsp grated orange rind
8 gelatin leaves*
1⅓ cups / 300 ml / ½ pint cream
4 oranges
1 cup / 250 ml / 8 fl oz orange juice

Bring the water to the boil, add the rice and cook for 10 minutes, then drain well.

Slit the vanilla pod lengthways and place in a pan with the milk and ⅔ cup/115 g/4 oz of the sugar. Bring to the boil, stirring until the sugar has dissolved, then add the rice and cook for a further 10 minutes. Remove the pan from the heat.

Remove the vanilla pod and add the orange rind.

Soak six gelatin leaves in a small bowl of cold water for 5 minutes. Remove the leaves and squeeze out the excess water, then dissolve in the hot rice mixture. Leave to cool.

Whip the cream until stiff and, as soon as the rice mixture begins to set, fold in.

Slice the oranges and divide among six serving dishes. Spoon over the rice mixture.

…continued

*see recipe notes page 4

Bavarois with
Rice and Oranges

Pour the orange juice into a pan, add the remaining sugar and bring to the boil, stirring until the sugar has dissolved. Soak the remaining gelatin leaves in a small bowl of cold water for 5 minutes. Remove the leaves, squeeze out the excess water and dissolve them in the warm orange juice. Divide among the dishes of rice dessert and chill in the refrigerator.

Tip:
You can also make this dessert using brown rice. In this case, the rice must be pre-cooked in boiling water for 40-50 minutes.

Italian Rice Cake

2 cups / 500 ml / 18 fl oz water
3/8 cup / 75 g / 3 oz long grain rice
2 cups / 500 ml / 18 fl oz milk
1/8 cup / 25 g / 1 oz butter, softened
1 tbsp semolina
4 eggs
5/8 cup / 115 g / 4 oz castor sugar
1 tbsp grated lemon rind
2 tbsp lemon juice
2 tbsp brandy
3 tbsp flaked almonds

Bring the water to the boil, add the rice and cook for 5 minutes, then drain well.

Grease an 11-in/28-cm gratin dish or pizza pan with the butter and sprinkle with the semolina. Preheat the oven to 180°C/350°F/Gas 4.

Bring the milk to the boil, add the rice and boil for 15 minutes, then remove the pan from the heat.

Beat the eggs with the sugar until pale and frothy. Stir in the lemon rind, lemon juice and brandy and stir. Fold this mixture into the rice.

...continued

Italian Rice Cake

Spoon the mixture into the prepared dish and smooth the surface. Sprinkle evenly with the flaked almonds and bake for 50-60 minutes.

The rice cake can be served hot or cold.

Tip:
Goes well with a fruit compote, such as plums or pears.

Rice Soufflé

2 cups / 500 ml / 18 fl oz water
3/8 cup / 75 g / 3 oz long grain rice
1/8 cup / 25 g / 1 oz butter or margarine,
   for greasing
1 vanilla pod
1 1/2 cups / 400 ml / 14 fl oz milk
pinch of salt
grated rind and juice of 1 lemon
1/4 cup / 50 g / 2 oz raisins
5 eggs, separated
3/8 cup / 75 g / 3 oz sugar

Preheat the oven to 180°C/350°F/Gas Mark 4.
Bring the water to the boil, add the rice and cook for 5 minutes, then drain well.

Grease a soufflé dish with the butter/margarine.

Slit the vanilla pod, place in a pan with the milk and the salt and bring to the boil. Add the rice and boil for 15 minutes. Remove from the heat.

Stir in the lemon rind and juice, then add the raisins and egg yolks.

Whisk the egg whites with the sugar in a clean grease-free bowl until stiff, then gently fold into the rice mixture. Turn the mixture into a soufflé dish and bake for 40-50 minutes.

Tip:
Serve with peach or plum compote.

Creamed Rice with Ginger and Raspberry Compote

6 gelatin leaves
1 quart / 1 liter / 1³/₄ pints water
⁵/₈ cup / 115 g / 4 oz long grain rice
2 cups / 500 ml / 18 fl oz milk
³/₈ cup / 75 g / 3 oz castor sugar
1 tsp grated lemon rind
¹/₄ cup / 75 g / 3 oz stem ginger, drained and
   chopped, plus 1 tbsp syrup from the jar
1¹/₃ cups / 300 ml / ¹/₂ pint double cream

Raspberry compote:
7 tbsp orange juice
2 tbsp clear honey
2 tsp arrowroot
2 cups / 300 g / 11 oz raspberries
2 fresh mint sprigs

Soak the gelatin in a small bowl of cold water.
Bring the measured water to the boil, add the rice
and cook for 10 minutes, then drain well.

Pour the milk into a pan, add the sugar and
bring to the boil, stirring until the sugar has
dissolved. Add the rice and boil for 10 minutes.
Then add the lemon rind, chopped ginger and
ginger syrup. Remove the gelatin leaves from the
bowl, squeeze out the excess water and dissolve in
the rice mixture. Leave to cool.

Whisk the cream until stiff and, as soon as the
rice mixture begins to set, gently fold it in. Divide
the mixture among dessert dishes and leave to set
in the refrigerator for several hours.

Pour the orange juice into a pan, add the honey
and bring to the boil. Mix the arrowroot with a
little cold water to a smooth paste and stir into the
orange juice mixture until thickened. Add the
raspberries, bring back to the boil, then remove

...continued

from the heat and leave to cool.

To serve, pour the raspberry compote onto the creamed rice and decorate with mint sprigs.

The Thai word for rice, khao, also means 'mealtime', which shows the huge importance of rice in Asia. The annual per capita consumption in Thailand is around 240 pounds / 110 kilos, while Canadians consume just 17 pounds / 8 kilos of rice a year.

Tip:
Cooking times for rice vary depending on the variety. The easiest way to check whether it is done is to scoop out a few grains with a spoon and bite them between your front teeth. They should feel just tender with no hint of grittiness.

Basic techniques for parfaits, sorbets and ice cream

Parfaits
The ice-making compartment of an ordinary refrigerator is adequate for making parfaits. Their relatively low water content means they will stay smooth.

Parfait mixtures are beaten in a heatproof bowl set over a pan of simmering water. This is the only way to ensure that the eggs bind without curdling.

Stirring the parfait mixture as it cools over a bowl of iced water prevents it from separating. Fast cooling also helps to prevent the development of salmonella and other micro-organisms.

Ice cream and sorbets
The best and easiest way to make ice cream and sorbets is in an ice-cream maker but if you do not have one, here's how to do it.

It is essential to prevent large ice crystals from forming, as they will spoil the texture and make the ice cream too hard. You can do this by beating the ice cream at least three times during freezing, at intervals of between 20 minutes and 1 hour. Pour the mixture into a plastic container and place it in the freezer for 1 hour, or until ice crystals are beginning to form around the edge. Turn the mixture into a bowl and beat well to break up the crystals, then return it to the container and freeze again. Repeat the process twice more at hourly intervals, then return the ice cream to the freezer until solid.

Finally, leave it to freeze completely. About 30 minutes before serving, remove from the freezer and allow to soften in the refrigerator, then stir until smooth. If required, cut into portions at this stage and return to the refrigerator.

Fair-Trade food

Coffee
Bananas
Rice
Tea
Chocolate
Cocoa
Sugar
Honey
Orange
 Juice
Flowers

All these ingredients are becoming widely available as fairly traded products. If you can't find them where you usually shop, please keep asking for them – it's worth visiting on-line shopping sites if you can and doing the same thing there as well. Even giant supermarket chains have to take note of what their customers want. This is a very important part of making trade fairer.

It's also useful to support alternative stores. Chain stores have enormous power over food producers – this is part of the problem with conventional 'free' trade. So shopping in smaller stores, or in the retail outlets of aid organizations, is a useful and often remarkably convenient way of finding fair-trade food. You're also supporting the organization in the process.

Fair-trade shopping does usually cost you a little more. This is partly because fair-trade producers are paid above and never below the cost of production. In recent years the price of almost all the food commodities exported from the South (or 'Third World') have been falling below what it costs farmers to produce them. As a result, farmers have been impoverished while traders and retailers have prospered, because they haven't cut the price you pay in the shops.

By keeping the price to producers above the costs of production, fair trade is now making a critical difference to the lives of many thousands of small farmers around the world. Some fair-trade organizations add a 'social premium', helping to fund schools or healthcare for everyone in the local community. There is also a commitment to buy at fair prices over a longer period, relieving some of the insecurity that plagues impoverished farmers, while allowing them to plan more confidently for the future.

Consumers get something extra for the price they pay, too. Fairly traded food is grown by small-scale farmers; rarely (except for tea) on plantations. Coffee, for example, is by its nature rather like wine, its flavor varying from region to region, even from farm to farm. Small-scale production preserves the variety of flavor and the quality of the product, which farmers care passionately about. It also allows for less use of chemicals, which are poisons for people as well as pests. Some fair-trade products are certified organic as well, and are the very best buy if you can find them.

The main reason for the price difference is, however, rather different. In rich countries industrial agriculture receives huge subsidies. For example, in 2002 President George W Bush increased subsidies to industrial agriculture in the United States by $90 billion – almost double what the UN says would eliminate the very worst kind of 'absolute' poverty from the entire world. The European Union also subsidizes its agriculture very heavily. If the same subsidies went to fair trade, the price difference with conventional trade would disappear – and poverty would be alleviated as well.

In poor countries the rules of 'free' trade, which prohibit subsidies and government intervention, are imposed rigorously – much more so than in the United States or Europe – by the World Trade Organization. The World Bank and International Monetary Fund meanwhile require indebted poor countries to export as much as possible to pay their debts. So they all export whatever they can sell – which frequently means tropical food products – at the same time. As a result there is a glut on world markets and prices fall.

The price difference between fair and conventional trade has little to do with efficiency, competition or better production methods – and everything to do with the exploitation of the relatively poor majority of the world's people.

Many poor countries have a shortage of food. Using their best land for food crops for export, whether fairly traded or not, may not look very sensible, especially if that means transporting them many thousands of miles. Dealing with the problems of food 'security' and protecting the world's environment will inevitably mean less globalization, more local consumption – in rich countries just as much as in poor ones. But it does not necessarily mean putting a stop to trade in food altogether. Products like coffee or tea cannot be grown outside the tropics. If trade becomes fairer for producers, and they are able to benefit more from it, they will eventually have more options to choose from.

As it is they have little or no choice at all. The lives of many millions of poor people currently depend upon growing the coffee, tea or bananas bought by consumers in the rich world. So long as the market is controlled by powerful food corporations like Nestlé, Unilever or Chiquita, and unfair 'free' trade is the norm, fair trade will remain an essential alternative. And, in the end, the only thing that prevents it replacing unfair 'free' trade altogether is the awareness of consumers, and their willingness to support it.

David Ransom
New Internationalist

Look for the label

What's 'fair' and what isn't? How can you be sure that a claim to be 'fair' is honestly made?

Conventional trade wants you to know as little as possible about how, where and by whom its products are made. Fair-traders want you to know as much as possible – in fact, the more you know the better. That is the most important single difference between the two kinds of trade. After all, the best guarantee you can have about what you buy is to be well-informed.

Even so, the claim to fairness is easily made, much harder to prove. There has to be some way of weeding out false claims and agreeing what is 'fair'. From time to time big food companies try to set up their very own 'fair' product lines and labels, which can be confusing and hard to tell from the real thing – that's one of the reasons why they do it.

So fair-traders – including producers – have been working together to develop a labelling system that sets down some basic standards and offers a guarantee. There are now registered fair-trade labels in North America, most of Europe, Japan and Australasia. To be sure that the product you want to buy really does conform to the basic principles of fair trade, check for the label before buying – and complain if any product makes the claim without the label.

Fair Trade Labelling Organizations International (FLO)

Most of the national fair-trade labels are now members of FLO, which is based in Germany. They have agreed common principles, which include:

- Democratic organization of production, in co-operatives and the like
- Unrestricted access to free trade unions
- No child labor
- Decent working conditions
- Environmental sustainability
- A price that covers the costs of production
- A social premium to improve conditions
- Long-term relationships

The FLO monitoring program ensures that all the trading partners continue to comply with fair-trade criteria and that individual producers benefit.

Most national fair-trade labels are now adopting the main elements of a common logo, which should become increasingly familiar to consumers around the world:

www.fairtrade.net

Britain
The Fairtrade Foundation:
www.fairtrade.org.uk

Canada
TransFair:
www.web.net/fairtrade

Europe
Max Havelaar:
www.maxhavelaar.nl

TransFair:
www.transfair.org

Ireland
Fairtrade Mark Ireland:
www.fair-mark.org

US
TransFair:
www.transfairusa.org

Japan
TransFair:
www.transfair-jp.com

Where to buy?

There's an enormous range of fair-trade products available from alternative outlets, most of which now sell food. Here the label matters less than the organization – whether it's an aid agency, an alternative trading organization (ATO) or a retailer that's made a clear commitment to fair trade.

The International Federation for Alternative Trade (IFAT)

This is a network of fair-trade organizations in 47 countries, many of them Southern producers. They have agreed common objectives:

- To improve the livelihoods of producers
- To promote development opportunities for disadvantaged producers
- To raise consumer awareness
- To set an example of partnership in trade
- To campaign for changes in conventional trade
- To protect human rights

www.ifat.org

Here are just a few IFAT members who sell some or all of the food products you will need for the recipes in this book:

Australia
Community Aid Abroad Trading:
www.caatrading.org.au

Britain
Traidcraft Exchange:
www. traidcraft.co.uk

Canada
Level Ground Trading Ltd:
www.levelground.com

Japan
Global Village Fair Trade Company:
www.globalvillage.org.jp

New Zealand/Aotearoa
Trade Aid Importers Ltd:
www.tradeaid.co.nz

US
Equal Exchange:
www.equalexchange.com

The Co-op (UK)
One large retailer that has made a serious commitment to fair trade as a matter of policy is the Co-op in Britain. It stocks all of the fair-trade ingredients you'll need for these recipes. The size of its outlets varies, from local 'convenience' stores to large supermarkets. All of them carry fair-trade tea, coffee and chocolate; you are more likely to find the others in the larger stores. Depending on where you live, you may be able to shop on-line.

Though smaller than the giant Tesco, Sainsburys and Asda (where fair-trade products are sometimes available as well), the Co-op does have stores around the country and in most larger towns. It has the advantage of being owned by its members, most of whom are also its customers. It is the largest farmer in Britain, so understands the point of view of the producer as well as the consumer.

Founded in the 19th century – when 'free' world trade was last as rampant as it is today – the Co-op is a reminder of the history and potential of progressive retailing. After a long decline, it is now experiencing a revival. Most countries have very similar co-operative retailers. If you haven't tried one of them recently, they're usually worth a visit.

www.co-op.co.uk

Fair trade – the contents
• In 2000, the retail value of Fairtrade Marked products in Britain was nearly US$50 million, up from US$4 million in 1994.
• Coffee was the biggest seller, followed by bananas, tea, chocolate and cocoa products, and honey.
• Around 120,000 workers and farmers in Latin America, the Caribbean, Africa and Asia benefited from sales of Fairtrade Marked products in Britain.
• There are 93 Fairtrade Marked products including cocoa, coffee, bananas, tea, sugar, chocolate, snacks, biscuits, honey and fruit juices available to customers in supermarkets and independent retailers, and 24 products are available from catering suppliers.
• Prices for robusta coffee beans crashed to 35-year lows on the London Futures market in August 2000. The price for arabica beans closed at nine-year lows in New York.
• In many Latin American countries, this meant it was no longer worth farmers even harvesting their beans. Many who did had to stockpile their crop and wait for better prices.

• Recently the world-market price for arabica coffee was 50.85 US cents per pound, compared to the Fairtrade price of 126 cents per pound.

Facts and figures

Prices
The prices of all the food commodities traded between the South ('Third World') and North have been falling sharply. The overall price index [Table 1] halved between 1980 and 2000, while the price of some individual commodities like cocoa and sugar [Table 2] have fallen very much further.

Table 1
Index of food and tropical beverages free-market prices: 1990 = 100

1980	164.1
1985	81.3
1990	100.0
1995	113.6
2000	84.5

Source: Handbook of Statistics, UNCTAD, 2001.

Table 2
Index of some tropical-food free-market prices: 1990 = 100

	1980	2000
Coffee	185.2	106.3
Bananas	72.1	80.9
Rice	151.0	71.0
Cocoa	204.7	69.8
Sugar	228.4	65.2

Source: Handbook of Statistics, UNCTAD, 2001.

Where they come from
Ever since people living in colder, Northern countries developed a taste for tropical foods the international trade in them has been very lucrative – but mostly for the dealers and retailers, rather than the producers. International trade in some commodities, like coffee and sugar, accounts for a large proportion of total production. Others, like rice, are also staple foods in their country of origin. Below are the biggest exporting countries today.

Table 3
Main exporters 1998-1999: value in US$ millions

	World	Top 3 exporters
Coffee & substitutes	14,313	Brazil 2,534
		Colombia 1,728
		Mexico 720
Rice	8,295	Thailand 2,025
		India 1,106
		China 788
Sugar and honey	12,272	Brazil 1,939
		Cuba 1,066
		Thailand 636

Source: Handbook of Statistics, UNCTAD, 2001.

The fair-trade 'niche'

Fair trade accounts for only a very small, if growing, proportion of total world trade. For coffee, total world production in 2002 was roughly 70 million metric tonnes, of which fair trade accounted for less than 16,000 metric tonnes of roasted coffee [Table 4]. So there is still a long way to go. The main consumers are in Europe: the Netherlands and Switzerland stand out for the level of fair-trade coffee consumption relative to their size [Table 5].

Table 4
Coffee: total sales of roasted fair-trade coffee, in metric tonnes 1998-2002

1998	11,663.8
1999	11,819.1
2000	12,818.0
2001	14,387.7
2002	15,779.9

Source: FLO

Table 5
Coffee: sales of fair-trade roasted coffee per country, in metric tonnes, 2002

Austria	409
Belgium	632
Canada	425
Denmark	655
Finland	109
France	1,387
Germany	2,942
Britain	2,079
Ireland	60
Italy	243
Japan	10
Luxembourg	68
Netherlands	3,140
Norway	232
Sweden	289
Switzerland	1,246
USA	1,854
TOTAL	15,780

Source: FLO

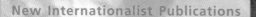

Index